MEGASTARS™

LADY GAGA

BRIDGET HEOS

rosen publishing's
rosen central®

New York

For hardworking and hard-dreaming artists everywhere

Published in 2011 by The Rosen Publishing Group, Inc.
29 East 21st Street, New York, NY 10010

First Edition

Library of Congress Cataloging-in-Publication Data

Heos, Bridget.
Lady Gaga / Bridget Heos. — 1st ed.
    p. cm. — (Megastars)
Includes bibliographical references, discography, and index.
ISBN 978-1-4358-3574-0 (library binding)
ISBN 978-1-4488-2260-7 (pbk.)
ISBN 978-1-4488-2266-9 (6-pack)
1. Lady Gaga—Juvenile literature. 2. Singers—United States—Biography—
Juvenile literature. I. Title.
ML3930.L13H46 2011
782.42164092–dc22
[B]

2010024138

Manufactured in the United States of America

CPSIA Compliance Information: Batch #W11YA: For further information, contact Rosen Publishing, New York, New York, at 1-800-237-9932.

On the cover: Lady Gaga, with her flamboyant costumes and obvious talent, has sold more than fifteen million albums.

CONTENTS

INTRODUCTION

In 2009, Lady Gaga burst onto the pop music scene with six hit singles on her first album. Who was she? A European star crossing over in America? A longtime musician finally getting radio play? An alien disco queen? In fact, she was twenty-three-year-old Stefani Germanotta from New York City. She may have seemed to come out of nowhere, but she had been working on her music and performance skills for years.

It all started when she was four years old and still known as Stefani. That's when she learned to play the

Lady Gaga performs at the Z100 Jingle Ball in New York City on December 12, 2008. At the time, she wasn't the household name that she is today. But she was working hard to get there.

piano by ear, meaning she could hear a song and then play the notes without looking at sheet music. She practiced hard at playing the piano. She also took acting lessons and tried out for every school play—often earning the starring role. Perhaps it is telling that, even backstage, she stayed in character. If her fellow actors called her Stefani, she would say, "No, I'm Adelaide," or whoever she was playing at the time.

Germanotta's music and drama studies didn't end after high school. She attended art school and then immersed herself in the New York City music scene. She listened to seventies rock, club music, and hard rock. She wrote everything from piano ballads to grunge rock. She also studied art, fashion, and fame. She'd been a hardworking student in school; now she devoured any lesson presented to her. If someone told her to look at a painting by Andy Warhol, she not only did that, but also read every book she could find about him, for instance.

Though she had listened to music and watched the performances of musicians past, she wasn't content to copy someone else. Instead, she created Lady Gaga, a modern disco queen who writes her own songs, creates over-the-top performances and videos, and wears avant-garde clothing. In a world of pop stars molded by record companies, Lady Gaga largely created herself by being a lifelong student of music, art, and fame.

CHAPTER 1

MANHATTAN

Stefani Joanne Angelina Germanotta was born on March 28, 1986, in Yonkers, New York, a city just north of New York City. She grew up in an apartment on the Upper West Side, a nice part of Manhattan. Her parents, Joseph and Cynthia, were first-generation Italian Americans. Her father was an entrepreneur in an Internet business. Her mother was a vice president at Verizon. They did well and were able to send Stefani and her younger sister, Natali, to Convent of the Sacred Heart, a Catholic girls' school on the Upper East Side of Manhattan. With its high academic standards (and high tuition), it has had some high-profile students, such as Caroline Kennedy and Paris and Nicky Hilton. Stefani's parents would remind her that they sacrificed for her education. She, in turn, worked hard and has said that attending Sacred Heart instilled in her discipline and a desire to learn.

Stefani's musical talents became apparent at an early age. She could play the piano by ear at age four. Seeing her potential, her parents encouraged her. Stefani went beyond the daily half-hour practice typically recommended by piano teachers. Instead, she practiced two hours a day. The hard work paid off. She wrote her first piano ballad at thirteen and played open-mike nights at the Songwriters Hall of Fame when she was fourteen.

Like many girls her age, she was interested in pop stars. Living in New York, Stefani was able to see them in person . . . at least from afar. In middle school, she and her friends would take the train

Lady Gaga plays the piano at Carnegie Hall in New York City on May 13, 2010. A piano protégé, she could play by ear by age four.

downtown and stand outside the building in Times Square where the MTV show *Total Request Live* was taped. They'd try to catch a glimpse of Britney Spears or 'N Sync. (Little did Stefani know that she would make an appearance on the show in August 2008, just three months before it ended.) When Stefani started her own high school band, however, it was her father's music that inspired her. He was a fan of classic rock, and her band covered acts like Pink Floyd and Jefferson Airplane.

In addition to music, Stefani was interested in acting. At age eleven, she took acting classes every Saturday. They taught her how to drink pretend coffee and feel pretend rain. In eighth grade, she began trying out for plays at the nearby boys' Catholic school, Regis High School. She often got the lead in musicals such as *Guys and Dolls*, in which she played Adelaide, a showgirl in love with a gambler, and *A Funny Thing Happened on the Way to the Forum*. Some girls, jealous of her being cast in the lead, called her "the germ." But Stefani was supportive of other singers and actors at the school.

Lady Gaga has said that she felt like a freak in high school. She told Ellen DeGeneres during a November 27, 2009, interview, "This is really who I am, and it took a long time to be OK with that." Other classmates have said that she was actually quite popular. Of course, a kid can be popular and still feel like a freak. He or she might feel different from the other kids, or might prefer to stand apart from the crowd.

As for Stefani's parents, they were traditional but supported their daughter's artistic pursuits. When Stefani made a demo of her love ballads, her parents passed copies of it out as favors at her sweet sixteen birthday party. Stefani's guests were impressed; they predicted she would become a star.

Cynthia Germanotta influenced her daughter's later interest in fashion. She owned a Chanel suit, and Stefani would watch her get ready in the morning, thinking she was the most put-together mother. (The usually outlandish Lady Gaga wore a Chanel suit during her "10 Most Fascinating People" interview with Barbara Walters in December 2009, as a tribute to her mother.)

Outside of high school, Stefani and her friends hung out at the Westside Restaurant, a diner in Manhattan. After school, Stefani waitressed and has said she was good at the job. She considered it to be part performance: she wore high heels, told stories, and created a romantic ambiance for couples. With the money she earned, she bought a Gucci purse, like the other girls at school had.

At the time, Stefani had brown hair and did ordinary things like go to school dances and hang out with friends, but her yearbook suggested an extraordinary future. Her dream was to headline at Madison Square Garden. Soon after high school, she set out to find fame.

LOWER EAST SIDE

After high school, Stefani attended New York University's prestigious Tisch School of the Arts. (Other graduates include actors Angelina Jolie and Michael C. Hall.) A drama student, she would take dance for five hours in the morning, followed by acting and singing classes. At night, she would study art. She loved her time in art school but began to feel like she could teach herself to be the artist she wanted to be. A year and a half after enrolling, she quit. She told her parents she wanted to be a rock star. Her dad agreed to pay her rent for a while, but she had to promise to reenroll if she wasn't successful by the time she turned twenty, in March 2006.

Stefani got an apartment on the Lower East Side of Manhattan, a neighborhood that is home to immigrants, artists, and musicians. She had a futon couch and a Yoko Ono record hanging over her bed. She dyed her brown hair black.

To make ends meet, Stefani worked as a waitress at the Cornelia Street Café and a dancer at the Slipper Room. Her father came to see her one night and was worried. His daughter, who had been a piano protégé, had quit school to dance in a leotard at a club—she wasn't even playing music. He thought she was mentally imbalanced.

Lady Gaga sings at the Grammy Awards on January 31, 2010, in Los Angeles, California. She started performing in plays and recitals in grade school.

LADY GAGA'S MANHATTAN

New York City is comprised of five boroughs. Manhattan is one of them. It is home to Wall Street, Times Square, Broadway, Central Park, and other New York landmarks. The Upper West Side, where Lady Gaga grew up, is a nice residential neighborhood. The Upper East Side, where she attended Sacred Heart, is an upscale neighborhood that encompasses Museum Mile and Madison Avenue. The Lower East Side, where Lady Gaga lived when she quit college, has historically been an immigrant neighborhood but is now home to many artists and musicians, too. It is near Chinatown, Little Italy, and Lower Manhattan, where Wall Street is located.

Sadly, he didn't speak to her for several months. This was heartbreaking to Stefani, who valued her dad's opinion over everybody else's. The two even had their own song, "Thunder Road," by Bruce Springsteen. Eventually, Stefani's father came to understand her artistic vision (he even got a tattoo of a lightning rod—signifying Lady Gaga's lightning eye makeup).

In spite of the dancing, Stefani was serious about her rock star ambitions. She performed with Mackin Pulsifier and the Stefani Germanotta Band, which she formed with friends from NYU. To get gigs, she would ride around town on her bike pretending to be the band's manager. This is how her band got booked at the Bitter End, a rock bar that Norah Jones, Tori Amos, and Stevie Wonder, among others, played in their early years.

The Stefani Germanotta Band had a following of about fifteen to twenty people, and sometimes other listeners would be at their shows, too. In 2005, the band's demo, *Words*, came out, but went nowhere. The next March, Stefani made her own demo, *Red and Blue*. It showcased her vocal and songwriting talents, but didn't have the unique style needed to stand out. Unfortunately, her dad's cutoff date was nearing. Would she have to kiss her dream of being a rock-and-roll star good-bye?

A week before her twentieth birthday, Stefani was performing at the Cutting Room in New York. So was a singer named Wendy Starland, who was working on tracks with producer Rob Fusari. Fusari, a thirty-eight year old from New Jersey, had worked on R&B hits for Will Smith and Destiny's Child. He had told Starland he wanted a female singer for a band like the Strokes. When Starland saw Stefani, she thought she was the plain-looking lead singer of a terrible band. But there was something about her. She had an amazing voice and energy. After the show, Starland found Stefani and said, "I'm about to change your life."

CHAPTER 2
FROM STEFANI TO GAGA

After Starland promised to change Stefani's life, the two walked outside the Cutting Room. Starland called Fusari and woke him. He asked what the singer looked like. Starland said not to worry about that. He asked whether she had any good songs. Starland said no. He asked about her band. Starland said it was terrible. But somehow, she convinced Fusari to let Stefani try out for him.

When Stefani arrived on Fusari's doorstep in New Jersey, he hoped she wasn't the girl Starland had sent him. She didn't look like a rock star. Skeptically, he let her play the piano for him. He was blown away. Her voice wasn't right for the band he was putting together, but she had a unique talent. She reminded him of a female John Lennon.

That spring, the then twenty year old Stefani would ride the bus to Fusari's house. They'd write music all day. At first, they worked on Nirvana-type grunge songs. But that didn't go anywhere. Piano ballads seemed like an obvious fit (she'd been writing them since age thirteen). But there were too many singer-songwriters out there, and Stefani didn't look right for the part.

Things turned around when Fusari read that producer Timbaland had helped transform Nelly Furtado from a singer of ballads (such as "I'm Like a Bird") into a dance artist. Gaga didn't like the idea at first, but agreed to work with a drum machine. She also began dating Fusari.

Queen included musicians Freddie Mercury (front center) and (left to right) Roger Taylor, John Deacon, and Brian May. Lady Gaga was named for the band's song "Radio Gaga."

WHO IS QUEEN?

Lady Gaga got her name from Queen, a British rock band that formed in 1971. They were known for their hard rock melodies and theatrical concerts. They even created a rock opera, which they called "Bohemian Rhapsody." Their songs include "Another One Bites the Dust," "We Will Rock You," "We Are the Champions," and, of course, "Radio Gaga."

He was the one who spawned the name Lady Gaga. Queen, a popular band in the 1970s and '80s, had a song called "Radio Gaga." It's about how important radio was before television and music videos. When the band's lead singer, Freddie Mercury, was a teenager, it taught him every-thing. He says that radio is still important, but now all he hears is "radio gaga"—gibberish. Stefani's theatrical voice reminded Fusari of Mercury. When she'd walk into the studio, he'd sing "Radio Gaga." There are several versions of what happened next. One is that Fusari e-mailed Stefani with "Radio Gaga" as the subject but that his spell check changed it to Lady Gaga. She liked the name, and it stuck. Another is that when she was playing a track called "Again, Again," Fusari said Stefani was "so Radio Gaga." She then added "Lady" to the nickname. Whatever the case, Lady Gaga was born.

At the time, she wasn't the Lady Gaga we know today. She was still a brunette. She dressed more casually—in leggings and a sweatshirt, for instance. Fusari has said that he told her she needed to dress up. If a music rep was in the studio, she'd make a bad first impression. He said Prince didn't even go to the convenience store in sweats; he was a rock star all the time. Always a student who went above and beyond, Lady Gaga not only absorbed that tidbit of advice but also read a biography of Prince. She began shopping at American Apparel, a store that, among other things, sells leotards and unitards, typically worn with a skirt or pants. Gaga began wearing short skirts and eventually just the leotard or leggings.

Together, Fusari and Gaga wrote the song "Beautiful, Dirty, Rich," which is about rich young adults asking their fathers for money. Lady Gaga has said it was based on students at NYU. The song attracted attention, and managers watched Gaga perform in a showcase in downtown New York. She was also invited to try out for Island Def Jam Records.

To Gaga's excitement, the president of Island Def Jam, L. A. Reid, signed her to an $850,000 record deal and told her she was going to be a star. But after she produced the tracks, her luck turned. Reid didn't return her phone calls. As it turned out, he didn't like her after all. Just three months after signing, she was off the label. ("Beautiful, Dirty, Rich" and another future hit song were on the never-released Def Jam record.)

When Gaga told Fusari that the deal had fallen through, she was sobbing. "I went back to my apartment on the Lower East Side, and I was so depressed," she told *New York* magazine in the March 28, 2010, issue. "That's when I started the real devotion to my music and art."

THE ART OF PERFORMING

Gaga and Fusari drifted apart. She started hanging out in the hard rock scene. She fell in love with Luc Carl, a drummer and manager of a rock bar. She also met Lady Starlight, a performance artist and hard rock fan. They performed in New York clubs as "Lady Gaga and the Starlight Revue: The Ultimate Pop Burlesque Rock Show." It was a tribute to 1970s variety acts. They also opened for glam rock bands such as the Semi Precious Metals. Before the shows, they would listen to David Bowie—a huge influence on Lady Gaga—and sew bikinis to wear as costumes. (The lightning paint Lady Gaga sometimes wears on her eyes is a tribute to Bowie.) Gaga also listened to club music like the Cure, the Pet Shop Boys, and the Scissor Sisters, which would influence her music as well.

Lady Gaga (left) and Lady Starlight practiced performance art onstage. They're seen here at a VMA party on September 13, 2009.

In a way, performing in bikinis seemed to be a step backward to Gaga's dancing days. But Lady Starlight was teaching Gaga to understand herself as a performance artist. (Performance artists act out sometimes bizarre scenes as art.) Her past dancing experience was now shaping her performances as Lady Gaga.

Not everybody saw it that way. Fusari wasn't impressed by Gaga's and Starlight's act. He told *New York* magazine (March 18, 2010) that "it was *Rocky Horror* meets eighties band, and I didn't get it at all . . . I told Stefani that I could get her another DJ, but she was like, 'I'm good.'"

Lady Gaga has said that David Bowie is one of her biggest influences. Born in London, England, Bowie became a 1970s rock icon with the album The Rise and Fall of Ziggy Stardust and the Spiders from Mars. *In it, he sang as his alter ego, the alien Ziggy Stardust. Like Queen, his performances were part theater and part concert. Like Lady Gaga, he wore outrageous clothing. His songs include "China Girl" and "Modern Love."*

Her father was also concerned. He suspected that his daughter was doing drugs. This may have been true. Stefani thought that in order to be an artist, she needed to go through a "drug phase." She later said this was completely unnecessary. But it's what she thought at the time. She would do drugs alone and listen to the Cure. This led to panic attacks. But she didn't stop—not yet. It took her dad's harsh words to get her to quit. He didn't mention the drugs directly but told her she was messing up her life. He said she would lose her friends if she kept this up. Stefani gave up drugs and realized that critical thinking was the path to creativity.

Some people are skeptical of the pop star's drug use story. Friends of hers have said they never saw her do drugs. (She told them she only did drugs alone.) Whatever the case, this was around the time that

David Bowie, a rock icon, is one of Lady Gaga's biggest influences. He's pictured here performing in the Netherlands on October 15, 2003.

her manager introduced her to RedOne, an internationally known producer. Born in Morocco, he moved to Sweden to be a part of the rock scene there. Much later, his song "Bamboo," performed by Shakira, became the official song of the 2006 FIFA World Cup.

When they met, Gaga and RedOne talked about David Bowie and Led Zeppelin. Then they went into the studio and wrote "Boys, Boys, Boys." He'd synthesize the beats and she'd sing the lyrics. He has said that, while working with Gaga, she's not just creating music. She's also thinking about the video and the performance. He compared her to a Michael Jackson or Madonna—an artist's artist.

But it was Fusari who got the attention of another record company. Fusari sent Gaga's music to Vincent Herbert of Streamline Records, which is distributed through Interscope. Herbert flew Gaga to Los Angeles, California, to meet with company chairman Jimmy Iovine. Iovine is known for having a good ear for music. He's worked with musicians in styles ranging from gangsta rap to soft metal.

When Iovine met Gaga, he thought, "I know her." He meant that he knew her type. She was a hardworking songwriter from Manhattan, like a Carole King, ("Will You Love Me Tomorrow") or Cynthia Weil ("You Lost That Lovin' Feeling"). He thought she might work out. Of course, he wasn't the first record executive to think that. This time, would it work out for Lady Gaga?

CHAPTER 3

THE FAME

In 2007, Lady Gaga began working at Interscope Records in Santa Monica, California. In addition to recording with RedOne, she wrote for other artists, including the Pussycat Dolls, the New Kids on the Block, and Britney Spears.

Lady Gaga performs at Lollapalooza in Chicago, Illinois, on August 4, 2007. Up to that point, her hair had been brown. After somebody mistook her for singer Amy Winehouse, she dyed it blond.

At this point, Lady Gaga's hair was still brown. That changed when Vincent Herbert of Streamline Records sent her to perform at the Lollapalooza festival in Chicago, Illinois. While she performed electronic dance music on a keyboard while wearing a bikini, somebody called out, "Amy Winehouse!" Winehouse is a blues/rock singer whose drug and alcohol addiction cut her rising music career short. The association made Herbert nervous. He told Gaga she should dye her hair blond. She did just that.

But she was still self-conscious about her looks. Though beautiful by most people's standards, she worried the label might not think she was pretty enough to perform. She worried she'd only be able to write songs for other people.

According to *New York* magazine, she told a friend that she was going to get a nose job. That friend suggested she look at Andy Warhol's "Before and After 1," a painting that depicts a woman

Andy Warhol, seen here on May 1, 1967, was an artist fascinated by fame. Lady Gaga studied him and began to see fame as an art form.

before and after a nose job. Lady Gaga went to the Metropolitan Museum of Art in New York to see it. In typical Gaga style, she didn't stop there. She read everything she could about Warhol. She highlighted passages she liked.

Andy Warhol is famous for saying, "In the future, everyone will be world famous for fifteen minutes" (a prediction that may come true, thanks to social media like YouTube and Facebook). He was not only fascinated with fame for everyone but also with movie stars. He created silk screens of teen idols Natalie Wood and Warren Beatty, and, after her death, Marilyn Monroe. He became a star himself in the 1960s, known for his pop art and the Factory, a group of artists that worked with him. He was a mysterious star, often telling reporters conflicting stories about where he came from and who he was.

Gaga was coming to understand that fame, in itself, was an art form. She thought about how obsessed her generation was with celebrities. She thought about how, even when stars got in trouble and took mug shots, they posed for the camera. She also thought about how, when she and her friends were performing and making art on the Lower East Side, they felt famous, even though they weren't. She decided to name her first album *The Fame*.

In episode twenty-seven of *Gagavision*, a Web series about Gaga's early days on the road, she says, "Fame is when everybody knows who you are. *The Fame* is when nobody knows who you are and everybody wants to know who you are." She said she hoped the album would inspire in others "the fame"—the feeling of inner confidence.

Interestingly, when the album was named, Lady Gaga was not famous. Instead, she seemed to be playing a role, just as she had in school plays: that of a so-called famous pop star. Soon, the act would come true. Only she has said Lady Gaga isn't an act. It's who she's always been. It's who she wakes up as. It's who she is when she visits her family. Stefani Germanotta *is* Lady Gaga.

Lady Gaga holds up the album The Fame Monster at a launch party on November 23, 2009, in Los Angeles, California. Many of her songs and performances focus on fame.

Or so the story goes. At times, where Stefani Germanotta ends and Lady Gaga begins is ambiguous. As Lady Gaga told *Out* in the September 2009, issue, "This isn't the Lady Gaga newscast. Nobody [cares] what is really going on. Everyone wants me to tell a story. Art is a lie, and every day I kill to make it true."

"Just Dance" was the first single on *The Fame* to be released. It came out before the album itself—in April 2008. Written by Lady Gaga and RedOne, "Just Dance" was the song that made Interscope believe in her. When Interscope's big artist, hip-hop and R&B sensation Akon, heard "Just Dance," he loved it. Because of his influence, Interscope lent more support to Gaga's upcoming album. She started recording at the home studio of top executive Martin Kierszenbaum and joined his Interscope label, Cherrytree Records. She also started Haus of Gaga—an art collective similar to Warhol's Factory. It is made up of managers, stylists, designers, and artists that Gaga is friends with or admires. Haus of Gaga helps Lady Gaga be Lady Gaga—complete with avant-garde hair, makeup, clothing, and set design.

All the pieces of Lady Gaga were falling into place. Now it was time to promote her first single. Like most other songs on *The Fame*, "Just Dance" is disco (more popularly known today as electropop). In Europe, where RedOne's music career had flourished, electropop had been popular for a long time. But in America, rap was the dance music of choice. (This explains why Gaga would top the charts in Europe before her native America.) RedOne believed that by writing electropop, he and Gaga could bridge the gap between America and other countries. He told *New York* magazine in March 2010 that "Gaga and I believe the world needs this music, that it is a way to unite."

With Lady Gaga's influence, electropop might grow more popular in America, bringing the country back to its disco days of the 1970s and '80s. But when "Just Dance" was first released, American radio stations weren't too keen on electropop songs.

JUST PLAY "JUST DANCE"

It may seem hard to believe now, but Lady Gaga and her crew had a hard time convincing radio stations to play "Just Dance." It was too different from what was popular at the time. To promote the song, she toured dance clubs around the country. Onstage, she had a DJ named Space Cowboy and two dancers wearing all black. (When she signed autographs, these dancers stood behind her, like bodyguards.)

"Just Dance" quickly became a hit in clubs. But it took longer to resonate with American radio listeners, let alone get airplay. In America, the song wouldn't become number 1 until January 2009.

Other countries were a different story. There, she was building on an already thriving electropop scene. When she left the United States to tour Canada in 2008, "Just Dance" and *The Fame* (released earlier in Canada than in the United

WHAT IS PERFORMANCE ART?

Lady Gaga and Lady Starlight practiced performance art in their shows. Performance art, which arose in the 1950s and grew more popular in the 1970s and '80s, is a work of art performed by people. An example is an artist onstage eating strange foods, such as Play-Doh shaped like monkeys. It is different from singing, dancing, and acting in that it is closely tied to avant-garde art (art outside the mainstream.) Lady Gaga and Lady Starlight were singing and dancing, but they were doing so as artists depicting people who were singing and dancing.

In a similar performance art piece, James Franco, who played Harry in Spider-Man, acted on the soap opera General Hospital. He wanted to see how viewers would respond to a well-known actor appearing in the fantasy world of a soap opera.

Lady Gaga dresses uniquely wherever she goes. She's pictured here on February 16, 2010, leaving the Mayfair Hotel in London, England, wearing one of her famously unique outfits.

States) were already number 1 in Canada. Later that year, she was off to Australia, where "Just Dance" had gone platinum. Finally, she headed to Sweden, where she played for a crowd of fifty thousand people who knew all her songs by heart. She spent weeks performing for Europe's adoring crowds.

Meanwhile, Lady Gaga started gaining traction in America. When Z100, an influential station in New York City played "Just Dance," other stations followed suit. "Just Dance" finally reached the Billboard 100 in August 2008. Lady Gaga began touring U.S. radio stations. She would show up in full Gaga gear—complete with her new signature hair bow, catsuit, sky-high heels, and multiple pairs of fake eyelashes. DJs would remark that other stars dressed casually in the studio, but Gaga said she always dressed this way.

In January 2009, "Just Dance" finally rose to the top of the U.S. charts. By that time, The Fame had been released in America and Lady Gaga had toured as the opening act for the New Kids on the Block. Still, she wasn't the star she is today. When Christina Aguilera was asked about Lady Gaga by the L.A. Times in November 2008, she said, "I'm not quite sure of who this person is, to be honest. I don't know if it is a man or a woman."

That may have been true in 2008. But soon, everybody would know who Lady Gaga was . . .

In 2009, Lady Gaga became the biggest pop star in America. "Poker Face," "Love Game," and "Paparazzi" joined "Just Dance" at the top of the charts. Lady Gaga was nominated for five Grammys for *The Fame*. In March, she went on her own American tour, the Fame Ball. Gaga also made the rounds on the talk show circuit, from *The View* to *The Late Show with David Letterman*.

As the new "It" girl in America, she was drawing comparisons to Madonna and Michael Jackson—the biggest pop stars of all time. Madonna and Michael Jackson played the fame game for decades. People wondered if Lady Gaga would do the same, fizzle out, or like many young stars, crack under pressure.

Lady Gaga believed these musings to be the dark side of celebrity obsession: people enjoyed watching stars rise, but also fall. She told *Elle* in the December 1, 2009, issue that she acted out her demise in videos and performances so that the public could see her downfall. That way, they wouldn't be curious as to what it would look like in real life. That's why, in her "Paparazzi" video, she is thrown from a balcony, and, at the 2009 MTV Music Awards, she sang, "I pray the fame won't take my life." Then she moved to the piano, and upon returning to center stage, was covered with fake blood. In the performance, she died onstage.

The "Paparazzi" video not only gave fans a glimpse of Gaga's demise, it also made her a favorite in the fashion world. Designers

Madonna, pictured here performing on January 1, 1983, has said that she sees herself in Lady Gaga. The two appeared together on an episode of Saturday Night Live in 2009.

called to ask if they could send her samples of their work. As her options expanded, she moved beyond leotards, tights, and blazers with shoulder pads. Her outfits became more outlandish, and she was always ready for the paparazzi to snap her photo.

For her Fame Ball tour, she wore her now famous bubble dress and sat at a bubble piano. During a July 2009 interview on a German television show, she donned a Kermit the Frog jacket and headband. That December, she met Queen Elizabeth in England wearing a red pleather dress with poufy princess sleeves and a red beaded eye mask painted on her face.

Gaga didn't dial down her outrageousness in 2010. For New York Fashion Week, she performed at the amfAR gala on February 10

Lady Gaga meets Queen Elizabeth II on December 7, 2009, in Blackpool, England. She was popular abroad before she topped the charts in America.

wearing a white beaded bikini and hat with beads pasted to her legs, stomach, and face. The same month, she showcased a lightning rod headpiece at the 2010 Grammy Awards. Her eyes were painted in a pink mask, making her look like a superhero. She sat in stark contrast to her dad—her date that night—who wore a subdued black suit and shirt.

Such outrageous outfits have drawn praise and criticism. In 2009, *People* named Lady Gaga one of fashion's best rebels. She explained her eclectic style to the magazine in its September 16, 2009, issue:

Lady Gaga plays at a bubble piano, wearing a bubble dress, in Sydney, Australia, on May 25, 2009. It was one of her favorite outfits.

"I'm inspired by '70s glam, decadence, skyscrapers, Madonna." *Us* magazine, on the other hand, named her one of 2009's worst-dressed stars. She explained why she doesn't wear mainstream attire in the December 16, 2009, issue: "A girl's got to use what she has, and I'm not going to make a guy drool the way a Britney video does." At times, the media simply put Lady Gaga in a category of her own. A September 13, 2009, *TMZ* headline read, "MTV VMA Fashions— Good, Bad, and Lady Gaga."

In spite of having an entire "factory" dedicated to her style, Lady Gaga didn't take herself too seriously. She poked fun at her fashion sense when she appeared on the October 4, 2009, episode of *Saturday Night Live*. In a skit, she wore her bubble dress and bumped into cast member Andy Samberg in the hall. He, too, was wearing a bubble dress and said he would have to change. When she said the outfit looked great on him, the two tried to kiss. Of course, the bubbles got in the way.

Good, bad, bizarre, or funny, Lady Gaga's attire definitely sets her apart from the crowd of young pop stars. But she's also building on the tradition of pop star fashion icons such as Michael Jackson and Madonna. Jackson ushered in the red leather jacket trend. Madonna inspired the fingerless glove and layered lace look. It's hard to guess what trend Lady Gaga might start. Could people be wearing tights, leotards, and eye masks in the next few years? Or could there be a Kermit trend around the bend?

THE FAME MONSTER

With *The Fame* topping the charts, Lady Gaga released a new single, "Bad Romance," in October 2009. Originally, the plan had been to rerelease *The Fame* with a bonus disc including "Bad Romance" and other songs. Instead, Lady Gaga released an entirely new album. *The Fame Monster* came out in November 2009 and included "Telephone," "The Monster," and the piano ballad "Speechless."

She told MTV during a November 23, 2009, interview that each song on the album represents a different fear or monster. For instance, "Speechless" is about her fear of her father dying. For several years, he had a heart condition. He told Lady Gaga's mother that instead of having surgery, he would let his life run its course. Lady Gaga was on tour at the time. Listening to him talk about this over the phone left her speechless. She thought his decision would kill him. She went to the studio and wrote the song as a plea to him to have surgery. To her relief, he did, and it went well. Her bond with her father was closer than ever.

"Dance in the Dark" is about the addiction monster. In it, Gaga says the names of beautiful women who died tragically, such as Marilyn Monroe, Sylvia Plath, and Judy Garland. She sings that together they'll be dancing in the dark because when people are watching, they fall apart. Again, this plays on the theme of stars rising, but also falling, in a public way. (The song is similar to the title of Bruce Springsteen's "Dancing in the Dark." Lady Gaga has said she's a big fan of his.)

Lady Gaga's parents, Cynthia and Joe Germanotta, attend a party in New York in 2010. "Speechless" is about Lady Gaga's fear of Joe dying.

To promote *The Fame Monster*, Lady Gaga continued on her whirlwind talk show tour, appearing on Barbara Walters's December 2009 "10 Most Fascinating People" special. She also went on a world tour called Monster Ball. She called it a musical, rather than a concert.

ICONS SUPPORT GAGA

Icons such as Bruce Springsteen, Madonna, and Cyndi Lauper have been supportive of the new icon on the block, Lady Gaga. Lauper told Gaga before a show, "You look good kid; go out there and take no prisoners" (as recalled by Lady Gaga on Gagavision). Madonna has said that she sees herself in Lady Gaga. And Bruce Springsteen is a fan, too.

At a concert in New Jersey, she told the story of when she first met Springsteen. After performing at a concert, a little girl asked Lady Gaga for her autograph. She followed the girl to her seat, where a group of girls sat. One of them asked her dad to take a picture of them with Lady Gaga. The man holding the camera was Bruce Springsteen. She told him that he was the rock star in the room, and the two hugged.

In the show, her friends are in New York trying to find the Monster Ball, only they get lost.

Like the storyline of a musical, the tour had ups and downs. In March 2010, Lady Gaga passed out three times during a New Zealand show. She attributed it to jetlag. Later that month, however, she was presented with a giant birthday cake onstage and a YouTube tribute video that her fans had made. She said it brought tears of joy to her eyes.

Meanwhile, in America, a problem was brewing. Fusari, who had cowritten and produced "Paparazzi" and other songs on *The Fame*, announced he was suing Gaga for $30 million. He said that Gaga and her father had signed a deal that would give him 20 percent of her career earnings and that she therefore owed him for merchandise and other sales.

Lady Gaga responded with a countersuit, saying that the agreement hadn't been a legal one. She also said she would let the case play out in the courts, not in the media. Instead, she focused her attention on her world Monster Ball tour and planning the U.S. portion of it. She kept her fans updated on her whirlwind schedule, lovingly calling them her little monsters. And, of course, she didn't give up on her art. She wrote new songs and worked with Haus of Gaga on all things creative.

With her dance beats, performance art, and outlandish outfits, Lady Gaga has been a pop culture innovator. And she's done it by being a lifelong student of art and the hardest-working pop star in show business. For this reason, she has said that she's not a role model as a person but is a role model for the process (of creating art.)

"I believe that everyone can do what I'm doing," she told *New York* magazine. "Everyone can access the parts of them that are great. I'm just a girl from New York City who decided to do this, after all. Rule the world! What's life worth living if you don't rule it?"

TIMELINE

1986 Lady Gaga is born Stefani Joanne Angelina Germanotta on March 28 in Yonkers, New York. At age four, Stefani learns to play piano by ear.

1997 Stefani takes her first acting class.

1999 Stefani writes her first piano ballad.

2000 She begins playing at open-mike night at the Songwriters Hall of Fame and acting in plays at a nearby Catholic boys' high school.

2003 Stefani gains admission to the prestigious Tisch School of the Arts.

2005 Stefani quits school to become a rock star. The Stefani Germanotta Band plays in New York music venues but gains little traction.

2006 Stefani is introduced to producer Rob Fusari. Together, they write the songs "Beautiful, Dirty, Rich" and "Paparazzi," among others. He coins the name Lady Gaga. Lady Gaga is signed, and quickly dropped, from Def Jam Records.

2007 Lady Gaga begins work at Interscope Records, where she writes "Boys, Boys, Boys," "Just Dance," and "Poker Face" with the producer RedOne. After being mistaken for Amy Winehouse at Lollapalooza, she dyes her hair blond.

2008 "Just Dance" is released and soars to the top of the charts in Australia, Canada, and Sweden. Gaga embarks on an American club tour and a world concert tour. *The Fame* is released.

2009 "Just Dance" reaches number 1 in America. It is soon joined by "Paparazzi," "Poker Face," and "Bad Romance." Gaga begins her Fame Ball tour. *The Fame Monster* is released.

2010 Lady Gaga goes on a world Monster Ball tour.

DISCOGRAPHY

2008 *Just Dance Featuring Colby O'Donis the Remixes* (Interscope Records)

2008 *Just Dance Remixes Part Two* (Interscope Records)

2008 *The Fame* (Interscope Records)

2008 *Poker Face Remixes* (Interscope Records)

2009 *The Fame Monster* (Interscope Records)

2009 *Bad Romance the Remixes* (Interscope Records)

2009 *Paparazzi Remixes* (Interscope Records)

2009 *Love Game Featuring Marilyn Manson* (Interscope Records)

2009 *Love Game the Remixes* (Interscope Records)

2009 *Love Game Robots to Mars Remix* (Interscope Records)

2010 *Poker Face/Speechless/Your Song Featuring Elton John Live from the 52nd Annual Grammy Awards* (Interscope Records)

2010 *Bad Romance the Remixes Part Two* (Interscope Records)

2010 *Lady Gaga and Beyoncé in Telephone the Remixes* (Interscope Records)

Lady Gaga poses with a copy of The Fame Monster at a signing on November 20, 2009.

ALBUM A musical recording that includes several songs.

BALLAD Originally, a type of folk poem with four-line stanzas of a certain meter, often set to music. In modern music, a slow, sentimental song.

CABARET A style of entertainment often performed at a dinner venue that includes song, dance, and comedy.

DESIGNER A person who creates clothing or costumes.

DISCO A type of dance music with a fast, repetitive beat and melodies that combine soul and Latin American music.

ELECTROPOP The contemporary style of disco music.

GLAM ROCK A type of band in which members wore glamorous and outrageous clothing, hair, and makeup, especially in 1970s England. The most popular artist in this genre was David Bowie.

HARD ROCK A contemporary offshoot of blues music with louder, faster beats.

HIP-HOP A movement that encompasses many arts, from graffiti to rap music to break dancing.

PERFORMANCE ART An acting out of a work of art by one or more people.

PRODUCER In music, the person who manages the making of an album or demo—from the recording session to the final product. This may include writing or choosing songs, hiring musicians, and finding a record label.

RECORD One or more songs recorded for later listening.

SINGER-SONGWRITER An artist who writes, sings, and plays his or her own songs, often as a solo artist.

SINGLE A song—possibly from an album—released for radio play or Internet downloading.

STYLIST A professional who helps people achieve the look they want.

FOR MORE INFORMATION

Andy Warhol Museum
117 Sandusky Street
Pittsburgh, PA 15212-5890
Web site: http://www.warhol.org
(412) 237-8300
The Andy Warhol Museum showcases the artist's work and teaches
    about his life.

Cherrytree Records
2220 Colorado Avenue
Santa Monica, CA 90404-3506
Web site: http://www.cherrytree.com
Cherrytree Records is the imprint that Lady Gaga records under
    within Interscope Records. It represents new artists.

FADO Performance Art Centre
448-401 Richmond Street West
Toronto, ON M5V 3A8
Canada
Web site: http://www.performanceart.ca
(416) 822-3219
FADO Performance Art Centre is a nonprofit artist-run center for
    performance art.

Interscope Records
2220 Colorado Avenue
Santa Monica, CA 90404-3506
Web site: http://www.interscope.com
(310) 865-1000

Interscope Records is a major U.S. music company that produces Lady Gaga's records.

Ontario College of Art & Design
100 McCaul Street
Toronto, ON M5T 1W1
Canada
Web site: http://www.ocad.ca
(416) 977-6000
Ontario College of Art & Design is Canada's "university of the imagination."

Tisch School of the Arts
721 Broadway
New York, NY 10003
Web site: http://www.tisch.nyu.edu
(212) 998-1800
Tisch School of the Arts is the art school affiliated with New York University.

WEB SITES

Due to the changing nature of Internet links, Rosen Publishing has developed an online list of Web sites related to the subject of this book. This site is updated regularly. Please use this link to access the list:

http://www.rosenlinks.com/mega/gaga

Cohn, Rachel, and David Levithan. *Nick & Norah's Infinite Playlist.* New York, NY: Knopf, 2008.

Edwards, Posy. *Lady Gaga: Me & You.* London, England: Orion, 2010.

Forget, Thomas. *David Bowie* (Rock & Roll Hall of Famers). New York, NY: Rosen Publishing Group, 2002.

Gnojewski, Carol. *Madonna: "Express Yourself."* Berkeley Heights, NJ: Enslow Publishers, 2007.

Jakobsen, Kathy. *My New York.* New York, NY: Little, Brown and Company, 2003.

Krumenauer, Heidi. *Lady Gaga* (Blue Banner Biographies). Hockessin, DE: Mitchell Lane Publishers, 2010.

Pericoli, Matteo. *Manhattan Within.* New York, NY: Random House, 2003.

Rafter, Dan, and Tess Fowler. *Fame: Lady Gaga.* Vancouver, WA: Bluewater Productions, 2010.

Shanes, Eric. *Andy Warhol* (Great Artists). New York, NY: Rosen Publishing Group, 2009.

BIBLIOGRAPHY

Dinh, James. "Lady Gaga Dishes on Revamped Monster Ball Tour." February 17, 2010. Retrieved April 18, 2010 (http://www.mtv.com/news/articles/1632101/20100217/lady_gaga.jhtml).

Duke, Allan. "Ex-boyfriend Sues Lady Gaga for $30.5 Million." CNN, March 19, 2010. Retrieved April 20, 2010 (http://www.cnn.com/2010/SHOWBIZ/Music/03/19/lady.gaza.lawsuit/index.html).

Frere-Jones, Sasha. "Ladies Wild." *New Yorker*, April 27, 2009. Retrieved April 16, 2010 (http://www.newyorker.com/arts/critics/musical/2009/04/27/090427crmu_music_frerejones).

Grigoriadis, Vanessa. "125 Minutes with Lady Gaga." *New York*, March 29, 2009. Retrieved March 25, 2010 (http://nymag.com/news/intelligencer/encounter/55653).

Herbert, Emily. *Lady Gaga: Behind the Fame*. New York, NY: Overlook Press, 2010.

Hiatt, Brian. "The Rise of Lady Gaga." *Rolling Stone*, June 11, 2009. Retrieved April 23, 2010 (http://www.thehausofgaga.com/articles/rolling-stone-magazine).

Kaufman, Gil. "Lady Gaga/Rob Fusari Lawsuit: A Closer Look." MTV, March 19, 2010. Retrieved April 19, 2010 (http://www.mtv.com/news/articles/1634292/20100319/lady_gaga.jhtml).

MSNBC. "Lady Gaga Is a Creation, but an Authentic One." June 29, 2009. Retrieved March 18, 2010 (http://www.msnbc.msn.com/id/31523496/ns/entertainment-music).

Stein, Joshua David, and Noah Michelson. "The Lady Is a Vamp." *Out*, September 2009. Retrieved April 18, 2010 (http://out.com/detail.asp?page=3&id=25720).

Vena, Jocelyn. "Lady Gaga Opens Up About Her Father's Heart Condition." MTV, October 27, 2009. Retrieved April 12, 2010 (http://www.mtv.com/news/articles/1624858/20091027/lady_gaga.jhtml).

INDEX

ABOUT THE AUTHOR

Bridget Heos is the author of several young adult nonfiction titles on topics ranging from biographies to science to states. She also writes picture books. Prior to being a children's book author, she was a newspaper reporter and freelance journalist. She lives in Kansas City with her husband and three sons.

PHOTO CREDITS

Cover, pp. 1, 4 Steve Granitz/WireImage/Getty Images; pp. 3 (top), 8 Kevin Kane/WireImage/Getty Images; pp. 3 (center), 11, 35 Larry Busacca/Getty Images; pp. 3 (bottom), 5 Scott Gries/Getty Images; p. 15 Terry O'Neill/Getty Images; p. 18 Amy Sussman/Getty Images; p. 20 AFP/Getty Images; p. 22 Jason Squires/WireImage/Getty Images; p. 23 Express Newspapers/Hulton Archive/Getty Images; p. 25 John Shearer/WireImage/Getty Images; p. 28 Neil Mockford/FilmMagic/Getty Images; p. 31 Dave Hogan/Getty Images; p. 32 WPA Pool/Getty Images; p. 33 Photo by Brendan Beirne/Rex USA, Courtesy of Everett Collection; p. 40 Kristian Dowling/Getty Images.

Designer: Nicole Russo; Editor: Bethany Bryan;
Photo Researcher: Karen Huang